News Worthy

First edition, 2026.

New York, New York, United States of America.

Photo by Nazlı Isguven

Published by McWest & Associates

ISBN: 978-1-971928-04-3

News Worthy

A Play about Journalism, War, and Moral Spectacle

Playwright by

Baruch Menache

Setting:

Contemporary. Time: the present day (early 21st century). Scenes may shift fluidly; lights, sound, and minimal props suggest location rather than full scenic realism.

On Language:

English. Occasional quoted dispatches, headlines, and fragments of foreign speech may appear; these should be comprehensible to the audience (either delivered in English, translated in text, or made otherwise intelligible). The language of the play balances plain, journalistic cadences with moments of intimate, lyrical speech.

Note: Directors are encouraged to center the humanity of the individuals offstage and resist voyeuristic spectacle in staging; focus on consequence, not sensation.

Dramatis Personae

STEVENS — A foreign correspondent; articulate, perceptive, and increasingly morally unmoored

RICK — Family friend; grounded, reflective

FATHER — An older man; unsettled by the moral drift of the world around him

SISTER — Young, lyrical, idealistic

YOUNG BROTHER — Intense, searching, drawn toward grand narratives

NIGHT WORKER — A woman Stevens meets in a hotel; perceptive, unsentimental, morally incisive

STRAGGLER — A man on the street; observant, ironic

BAKER — A neighborhood baker; practical, rooted

ASSISTANT BAKER — Fierce, outspoken, morally charged

COLLEAGUE — Fellow journalist; sharp, ideological, argumentative

CHIEF EDITOR — Authority figure in the newsroom

DESTITUTE MAN — Civilian in a war-torn country; weary, searching to be heard

REBEL SOLDIER — Fighter in the conflict; performative, eager for recognition

ENEMY — Opposing fighter; equally convinced of moral claim

ASSISTANT — Stevens's field assistant

ABDUL — Local man in the conflict zone; philosophical, wary, morally grounded

DAUGHTER (voice) — Stevens's child, heard by phone; innocent yet forming her own identity

CHORUS — Voices of memory, culture, and collective history; may be played by multiple actors

Act I: Summer

*[Summer barbecue, backyard friends and family, older man who is a
family friend speaks to his friend, Stevens, who is a foreign reporter]*

<u>*RICK*</u>

Disrupt my sober smile,

An unbearable dread

Made happy in the outback

Spine chilled to a morning glaze.

[His friend]

<u>*STEVENS*</u>

[Reporting on what he saw on his last assignment]
Reaping crop on snowed ground,

Stick figure; cold'n flesh and rock fingers,

Row by row, hill by hill, valley by valley;

Cleared path for a better coat of ice.

Squash season do not forgive so easy,

Crop be good—give it a twist.

Smile, that'll feed hunger 'n pickin' food;

Chicken and rooster must eat,

Stallion and his dire fill.

Workers done good by the pound,

Merry in diluted soup and cow's scraps.

<u>*RICK*</u>
Framed the wrong way—
Dispersed feelings onto empires,
Shadowed illusion of the feral man
Tracking small steps with baby shoes.

Coming with a loaded story of East,
Spice Age bears the same dreary tales,
Silken road of harbingers and a Roman coin,
Only for certain it is not your clan,
Neck-deep in a pile of another's mess.

[Olden Father is disturbed]

<u>*FATHER*</u>
Fresh barbecue to olden men,
Leisure to children's passage.
Joy mixed with happiness
Tells the scavenger hunt—
With no colored eggs,
No carved pumpkins—
Dare no jingle or drop.

[Young sister overhears and joins in]

<u>SISTER</u>
Maiden's basket overflowing fruit
Smiling her way to sunset road
As if summer don't end,
Then we know it doesn't—not ever,
A thousand ice age hasten grip.
Shan't shade be banned from existence?
Dare say a word about winter and be exiled.

<u>STEVENS</u>
Tale of sight does no agony rest
Baffles the ear drum as the left toe,
Simmers when crisp morning dawns away,
Fogs the mist arraigned for a protracted day.

<u>YOUNG BROTHER</u>
Felt the fright of newness
In a place that isn't yours.
Sell a wager of antiquity
To commence a revolution.

Whence convince soldiers of men
To grab spear and tools of trade
Toward a memory promising a fade.

That'll be a pound of flesh for two minutes of
memory, sir.

Hey, you! Back of the line!—your two minutes
ain't yet,

Ah, revelation he's told, the way he forgets
mother's kiss

But a hundred paces for a skinny relic.

Shock and awe will tell ya, there's no other way—
is there?

All avenues been explored, gory is all that's left,

So spear your fellow and take charge of the
memory.

STEVENS

Much to learn, young one,

Great traits of man are finitude,

Destitute is rather a future uncritical.

Telling a tale backwards is no tale at all,

To be God and man is no trait of God.

Be a mister or a maiden, be chancellor or subject,

Be devil or angel—flap or swim, jump or skip

But do not, my dear young one—

Do not award praise and condemnation in a single
breath;

Dare eat nourishment without questioning its
source,

Sleep to be aware of the awaken.

<u>*YOUNG BROTHER*</u>

Thought is weighty on my mind,
I'll speak when words are choosin'
Till then we remain in those words,
Wrong to be corrected or else to the soul.

Good Day.

<u>*STEVENS*</u>

You too.

[Night fades out, everyone slowly leaves]

Act II: Hotel Room

[After intercourse with a night worker, she is preparing to leave]

NIGHT WORKER

Rabbit furs are delightful treats

Cast around warm necks,

Softenin' elbows 'gainst crass wool;

Swiftly grants white her sacred color

That no paint or dye may embellish.

[Staring in the mirror with him behind her]

Lady of the night must encase in such furs

To keep still the jitters that arrive thereafter.

She enrobes in silk Egyptian colors;

Concrete walkways to obliterate the deed.

Tomorrow's appointment nearing,

A second shower—to be slowly fed,

Coddled by nimble arms 'n taking coffee late

All laden in priestly rabbit furs.

STEVENS

Flamingos in earthly flight,
There's a lover to catch;
Thy love will be second chanc'd
Passed by a first encounter;
A sweet thing dost regale in quiet.

NIGHT WORKER

Champagne glass and the unsuspecting lady
Merge to disdain a French countryside.
Feeling as ought to be,
Stage one of its downfall
That'll never see it coming,
Warrant defense to belated preparatory.

Cherished photo of pain,
I'd say for peace—for accountability;
The wink will come, erotic of bullets.
I am made of mischief without morals,
Dare look at me, look at what I'm saying.

[In regards to his occupation, seeing his editorial]
Report to the freedom of words,
Report thy cling to detestable life,
I'll do one better than thy savior,
I'll be sufferings' witness share;
Freedom to embark the black hole,

Anything but thy neighbor's wife,

Anything at all but foulness of breath,

That'll smell of lady in the night.

Get a head clear 'fore you speak of blood.

STEVENS

Talk the motion of your trade,

Blasphemous to thy namesake;

Spring advice from a sheltered rock

Raptured for sin to tell right from wrong;

Undignified can call the unseemed life.

[She leaves somewhat upset, then he sleeps]

Act III: The Street

[EARLY MORNING, ON THE STREET IN THE CITY]

[Awakes very early, takes a walk—on the road, street people begin to gawk]

STRAGGLER

My, my, look here at new folk,

Desperatin' to impress any 'nd all;

Silky ties and shiny shoes,

Removes the coveted mystery;

Covers the stench of work

In overbearing loads.

Half a paycheck in wearables,

A quarter in that smile.

STEVENS

Worked the same job, giddy in deterrence,

Sailed the current, happiest—five minutes out.

Risk adverse is a second-rate circus;

First place—sold man for man.

Chains of bondage is the trapeze

To crowds who await injury,

All solemn in the ritual of pain.
Victorious is he with camera in hand
For the next viewing to take to task,
Explained details in a digital copy.

STRAGGLER

An abundance of wit and charm
Is the remainder of a happy child.
Wear and tear is man of today
Except ever a good first use.

STEVENS

Try the conscripter who made the designs,
Seeing the universe in a single man,
Dost burden man, God and the universe.
Awfully mystical to expound man's sins
If only sin discussed that we may hash out,
Rather envy inscribed on thy forehead
Grants mystical know-how in my being;
Truss the tails of omnipresence in my haggard
suit.

Act IV: Bakery

BAKER

Came in for rolls, buttered to the next flip,

Scratched the surface of good men's heart.

All ya see is blood and sin

Goes the trip that flies two-way,

Awaiting man and the one-way ticket,

Called a destination 'n found at last.

Swinging in the air like fowl mid-flight

Thinking they know the city by over-sight,

As if sight, an admission to true tale.

Campfire and the spoken word,

Than believe sight is the bulkhead;

Thirsty to taste what is banned from bird 'n crow.

STEVENS

Treasured this stance in a cloud of flour

Thinking it'll be the same as dust of the Apache,

Claiming to be wise 'n furthest text—a Bible,

Even with some devouring gaps.

Tracing the mill to the spin of folks' tongue.

Training the most sounding word
As tip of spear in intelligent wear;
Spoken as a child never crossing the adult.

[Baker is embarrassed, tends to an arbitrary task, assistant baker becomes enraged]

<u>*ASSISTANT BAKER*</u>

All great advance in playing pawns as another's move,
Played the hand of God 'n confident fingers,
Is the great bitter before an ice age.
Who thinks to destroy yet short of remedy,
Who can flirt faster than a groping hand,
Even mocks the share grip of prowess
Not knowing midwives birthed better than chief surgeon,
Slip a thousand-and-one babes in the course of chisel and saw,
Ripping flesh and bone to extract the tired babe
Who needs more air than earth's supply.

[Baker joins in]

<u>*STEVENS*</u>

Bring the bread that is your occupation,
Roles picked by a deeming market,
Make fresh bread and fresher news,
Try your might at yeasted delights,

I'll finesse the better news to print.
The press will outdo bake only in word
But you-——a baker, words are not baked or rolled,
Stay nourished and speak less to prove words
vain.

[Baker and Assistant smile]

<u>BAKER</u>

Take care now.

<u>ASSISTANT BAKER</u>

Stay warm in the forecasted snow.

<u>STEVENS</u>

Gentleman.

[He bows and leaves]

Act V: The Office

STEVENS

Get the union worker who thinks he's the Eiffel
Tower,

Waging hours promised a lifetime of litigation;

With each screw, huff—bolt, a tuss,

Coddled just so to make a working man trod and
falter,

Banned from city limits goes the complaining
farmer who don't do crop without blowback.

COLLEAGUE

Sincerity left the stage to go for a mark at news,

Planned the revolution by spin-wheeling free
gossip,

Taken stage of a neighbors' trust,

Fiddled the remorse of a bashful lie,

Spoken of humanity to forget next of kin,

Paper to spread walls thin and kettles cold;

Namesake to an information dynasty,

Scraps of a diner as its last patron walks.

STEVENS

Why so righteous to gawker and complainer?
Prop the lowly is a deserter's cause;
Trust and fair word contradict,
Spake the white tale of fortune,
One of great tragedy and demise.
Suppose a mythical tale of moral,
Great strides or struggle inconsequential.
Sevenfold crimes of chickens
Laying eggs to the despondent;
Threefold to the grace of sheep,
Shearing wool for a new season.

COLLEAGUE

Let's go at a play at God,
Eve's square ball is a laden trust,
Chief Editor to square all mind to line,
Gift of freedom to teach mother her cooking,
That a child may ask for more 'bruschetta'
And forget his first, second and third meal.

Tell the tainted working man his fellow,
Find the detestable agony of plight,
Tell of rich and powerful to glee all night.

[Chief editorial walks past, changed the subject to talk about the next assignment]

Barbarism as its worst than

Respectful folk doing the dirty.

The televised spectacle is the unredeemed slay,

Copied for archives is worthwhile in failures,

That'll allow many-a-time—

Emptied cannons with no digital witness,

A great archival to fill a database,

Slots of entry to human empathy,

Over-told in gym lockers for simulacra

To keep from sending metal to a neighbor's reserve;

Afloat the daily currency of needed sweat,

Discharged in feudal lands and redeeming hands.

<u>STEVENS</u>

Allow me to tell a story as narratives float,

Critiquing the process never proceeds;

Better accounting that'll give service,

If the inferno is not enough for a single page

A double will cross the editor desk,

Triple—the politician's luncheon.

In the space between friendly and banter,

Holding remorseful spirit and good engineering,

Good 'gainst evil say evil will admit,
Only the bitter withhold admittance.
Crime only told by the lazy,
Half-dressed actor to a stage act,
Spew of politic and child antic,
Away dost dignity of children go,
Bespoken by the near-miss actor,
Who just needs to say the words,
Forgetting thy livelihood on the tithe
Of laborers and corporate men,
To alight the pig right out-the sty.

Betray the church choir's basket,
To give men a remorse for life
In half-truths and composition of sadness
Let the meager man tend to the sacrifice;
The angels and the devil are waiting,
Dost so righteous to hold the queue of
frankincense?
Dost fight man and god that evil will not wage?

COLLEAGUE

Report the objection of truth,
Mongers of pain with scripture told to scalps,
Jury-pool set on destroying fright,
To laugh is enough of the righteous,

Serious is the determinate fate,
Chasing her oblong shapes and deciding her rate,
Stock her as delirium and be psych worth,
Little episodic bate for symptom trait,
Goes the screaming child that hadn't conflict,
Goes the crocodile in Florida swamps,
Goes the flagship enterprise to dust,
Goes the jailed mother, slain'd father,
Goes forward with a burning tail,
Laughs the agent's slip on ice;
A laughing stock of hell's frontlines.

STEVENS

Face differing name goes the darkened twist,
I'd ponder as given the right to do so.
Smeared a campaign of horror,
Detestable existence is free wordplay,
Shared the yoke of indeterminacy
As if balance was a stage room,
Flickering light-shine of the endowment;
Two tell a story better than a bitter one.

COLLEAGUE

Torn to speak and see pain'd spirit,
A-masked of veneered trouble,
Be the church chasing wildflower,

Edward and Charles of worn sonnets,
No different thy oppressor or victim;
Preaching or sustained preached,
Budded fruit or pressed juice,
Sand or blown-glass-pigeons.

[Stevens shrugs his shoulders]

[Colleague turns sad and gives in]
Waiting for the forever in shadows-first,
Must I come and risk sunburn?
Forever will be tainted by a rising sun
Under the umbrella and never know light.

<u>*STEVENS*</u>

Don't think the mongers of walled ideas,
Go abase the nature of man—
In that spirit he's formed,
Blankets and bedding with less light,
Spirit of man trusses between pillow and weaning
hours.

Till we see each other in the confines of the other.

[He departs on his reporting duty]

Act VI: Reporting

[REPORTING IN A WAR-TORN COUNTRY]

[Sat down for an impromptu interview]

DESTITUTE MAN

Let me see those eyes glistening hope

Scarlet red as ruby in a black market

Clothed in stained hemp and dusty palms,

Told 'em worth of the big city and a great Mr.;

The only Mr. of this warring continent.

Given bloodshed a name, titled a history page.

Touch your fingers, may I?—stronger than a
mortar shell,

Myths begin the inscription

To last two more millenniums;

Smile worth all domestic product.

STEVENS

Tell me again, who are you?

At what corner?—what alleyway?

What was the sight, the color, the stream of
thoughts?

How'd you feel?—I'm the first and last to ask, do
you consent your rights?

After our short word, you'll do battle, won't you?

Get a front line view——need not return,

For your country, it's your must!

What a horror this mess is,

A black 'n white for the Johnsons,

Kids' school and this sir's plight.

Now, before you depart, tell me,

Where was your mother, your brother?

Fortified walls bearing your pain,

All locked in that cage of yours,

I'll tell you how misery is to be,

Confess your sins, show me a way!

[Answers the phone mid-interview—his daughter]

Pink or purple? Yes, it must be pink.

Troubled adolescent brings fashion distaste

Stalemate to nature's reluctance

Foraging emotionative fields as a cotton picking season

What are you gonna find, dear, do you think it will be better?

Chasing the devil never brought one closer to a resolve,

Dear, admit human's disparaging features and move along.

Daughter

Friends abash at last year's style,
Purple was the color of sixth grade,
Upped the place, and ranking so,
Let pink shine does a lady with edge.
Purple is momma's choice,
Doesn't she know pink is best?

I'll take the path carved in my own insolence
Than I'll know for sure that you and I are one,
Thrown to the pit of wolves does demand grit,
Even if salvation is always waiting around the
bend,
And grit and the misstep is my platform all robed
in pink.

Stevens

Mother lives by lazy color purple,
Clothed in that bluish hue
Won't tear down ever.
Between us dost reveal color pink
As the ancients never could do,
Make your choice for that new grade,
Pride yourself in the spread of a wing.

<u>*DAUGHTER*</u>

Pink it is.

[Hangs up the phone]

[Continues the interview]
Scatter the effect in a great moan,
Trounce your brother, give up friends.
Tell me all, don't stop for a minute,
Give me a tale of woe,
Something to print in black and white;
News at a deadline, give it now!
Deadline passed, give now!
Too late! Morning news be dry,
Get on with it, tell me your pain, tell it all.

<u>*DESTITUTE MAN*</u>

I'll give it all, should I be older? Taller?
Agony, yes, very much so,
I don't want to grieve you though.
Grandkids will hear this occasion,
Offer enough or too much?
Robbers, stealers, evil folk,
Taking fish from all seas, vegetation from all grounds,
All pretty girls broken of first rate blush,
It is them who ruined my love and romance.

Took my job, ruined the currency

Did I say stolen? Stolen everything I had,

Even what I did not,

Made stealable and stole them more.

All suffering is them, all pain is their doing,

The story is all, and there is no rest.

[Rebel Soldier passes]

<u>REBEL SOLDIER</u>

Hey, Destitute Man, it's time for your shift in
mud.

Need some sit down to talk of pain,

Take the weapon filled to half;

There's more pain to give.

[Turning to the reporter]

I am broken too, you should hear all they did.

Took my gun in an attempt to shoot,

Watched as we must follow the rules,

Disgraced the family name

By sharing the pot of remorse.

<u>STEVENS</u>

Sit here, more the merrier to the clan,

Never do know who is who,

Name your cause, or better, state your pain.

REBEL SOLDIER

Got some prints to show you, looks good to print overseas.

STEVENS

Great, did you get an angle?

A picture, perhaps, something carny?

No, no, not that much, respectful folk read 'em tidbits.

How about we schedule the battle in good lighting,

Could that be arranged, over that hill, what a great shot!

[Enemy passes by]

ENEMY

May I have a turn, those troubling western folk cause disarray.

Let the bicker of families with no charge,

Invoking domestic law the manner of ancient,

To no account of the numbers, towns even!

Family dispute is a fathers' love as a shared portion.

To have them come and tell us these morals.

Have no chance but to turn cotton into iron,

Choiced me into this game of mice.

Let's schedule the fighting before your departure,

A shame of good savagery with no English awe.

<u>*REBEL SOLDIER*</u>

Told him good lighting too,

Or we can take another shot at noon.

How's the mustache, pairs well with the funnies?

<u>*STEVENS*</u>

Lovely stuff, gentleman,

Got to go now.

[To his assistance]

Get us on the bound trip home,

Got my filling of these desert folk.

Act VII: War Scene

[STEVENS, ASSISTANT AND TWO OTHER COLLEAGUES,
THREE SECURITY MEN, AMIDST A SHOOTOUT]

[To the assistant]

STEVENS

Give a 35, a wide angle—did I say wide?

A cloth—now!—on the lens,

Dirty up the shot, what good is the picture?
Where's my video, get 'em video, they're gonna
eat this up.

Is that who I think it is?

Gerry, get on this, guess who showed up?

You wouldn't believe it.

No, I prefer cold brews, there's something thick
'bout them, what! What did ya say?

Cappuccino? European much?

Hey, Muhammad, what ya' think, an American
with a cappuccino?

ABDUL

Sister wives do no good for a man with camera,

Feeling the out-of-sight and near close to hell,

Be it the waters between waters, or the slain'd
preacher.

Have you come far as a mission of faith?

Or despite the headlong do you keep another eye?

Peeking the other way it could've went,

Salt to a wound, warning to your breed.

Let us sit in this mess of good Abraham,

Rebel the spirit of Rome to many-a-fall,

Be gone to merry land and forget this,

Earn me the right of passage over barbecue folk.

[Turning to the rest of the entourage]

STEVENS

Tribal yearning is the forbidden taste,

Can't play sand and not be child reared,

Merry-go-around and be passenger bound,

Offered the child a sense

That two worlds build 'stead of one.

ABDUL

Forgiven after shards of glass create a crystal vase;

Plan of action fails the ritualistic turn,

Speaking cryptic that'll calm the heart.

Panged at the price of one,

Destroyed in the least mannerly,

Awaits the trail of the bygone,

Tearing a misdeed from great injustice,

That too is marksman territory,

Three inches from the target center.

STEVENS

Join the ranks of the diabolical and delirious,

Told of a scout in the East who makes great
meatloaf—

Tell problems how often they come,

Sits in stew and tea, both simmering with angst.

Trouble you, kind sir, for some potatoes,

I'll take the lot and then some—

Starchy lovers all coddled in warmth of last
seasons' residue.

ABDUL

Come out of shadows and admit misfortune,

Wear black for an occasion or two,

Try the dirt path that we can see you dirtying,

Satisfied in the lot of infancy,

As though mothers' milk had no source,

Come yeast the rebellion that will lose the fight,

Make an entry when no exits to be found.

Sit in your soup and ladle, children and table,

Smile at the lot of men who breed less-so men,

Till soup and ladle are gone—

Stories old, recipes sickly, love piecemeal,
tenderness stage play;

Then what you men gonna do?

<u>*STEVENS*</u>

Sat in a pool of delirium and stubbornly,

Chosen the occupation of least rummage.

Pelicans sift the snow covered ledge.

[He leaves]

Act VIII: The Plane

[In a deep state of melancholy, muttering to himself]

STEVENS

Scrawny fellas in state's disguise,

Talking' over radio static,

Being frank about frankincense,

Pleasing the destiny of country will,

Handling of mongers in checkers,

Devout-will of the Christian faith,

Turned uphill to give the talky-talk,

Swearing their way to paradise,

Shortcuts to the rich fantasy,

For the state's love, its endearment of dowry,

Laden in forgotten grace;

Strange that exile is so near,

Scrapped together in a broken prophecy;

An untaught deal is a sentence of mind.

[As he lands]

Bank of thieves, spit-rolling,

Turn around the trade;
Showcase a one-pointer or fortune teller
To make amends with a nation and its currency.
To sit on a throne of paper, glass and sandcastles
With an army of stick figures and false
realizations,
Sentimental value carving a relic of the past.
This is your fortune, my friend;
Don't waste it on sentimental men.
The stranger you think
When knowledge is dumbfounded.

Act IX: Returns Home

[Entering his house]

CHORUS

In darkened rooms thy spirit sits,

Maiden to the men abroad,

Chiseled into rock of curves,

Sweet thing, she is—that her, says so,

Sapphire emboldened likeness,

Warmed cake to sweet tears and new holidays,

"We'll call him Timothy—

after your grandfather"

Psalms played into house acting

Where gained credit has no currency,

Currency is sacrifice to the tune of love.

Epilogue: Museum

CHORUS

The museum!

Child, look here, this is where man took his first steps.

A tyrannosaurus with all its bones intact, amazing!

Child look here, this is the great past,

Child look at this—man went to the moon.

What a mastery with all these feats!

Keep up now, there is so much to see,

Stay the course, you'll never get through it all.

Don't you care about these wonderful things? Grandfather would be proud.

Hey look here at this shiny thing, sir what's this called, this thing on display, right over here?

Tell me now, my child needs to know,

He came all this way,

He needs to know!

-The End-

About the Author:

43

Baruch Menache writes at the intersection of narrative, philosophy, and lyric expression. His work spans poetry, essays, and theatrical pieces that examine the interior life and its many thresholds. He lives in New York with his wife and children.

Other Playwrights

GIFTED WARES

A Lyrical Tragedy of Memory, Guilt, and Inherited Violence

FESTIVAL OF DOOM

A Poetic Drama of Friendship, Love, and Betrayal

TWITCHING HOUR

An Evening in Several Acts

GONE WEST

A Tragedy in Verse

www.ingramcontent.com/pod-product-compliance
Lightning Source LLC
Chambersburg PA
CBHW051415050726
47595CB00010B/4076